THE HOPE THE WORLD SMILES

Mohammad Ehsaar

THE HOPE THE WORLD SMILES

iUniverse books may be ordered through booksellers or by contacting:

iUniverse
1663 Liberty Drive
Bloomington, IN 47403
www.iuniverse.com
1-800-Authors (1-800-288-4677)

ISBN: 978-1-5320-3208-0 (sc)
ISBN: 978-1-5320-3209-7 (e)

Library of Congress Control Number: 2017913703

Print information available on the last page.

iUniverse rev. date: 09/20/2017

To the souls of my parents. May God bestow
on them His mercy and blessings.

To all friends and colleagues at my school,
and to all women and men,
I humbly dedicate this work.

Contents

I. Hope

1- *Definition*

Hope is the power to move all of your accomplishments forward. It is the basis that makes us think of endless possibilities. It is the motivation to find solutions to problems. It gives opportunity for accomplishments.

Don't stop when you are tired—stop when you are done!

2- <u>*Types of Hope*</u>

a) *Imaginary Hope*

Imaginary hope is the type of hope that remains in the mind only. No action is followed, and neither will it become reality. A majority of society possesses this type of hope.

b) *Realistic Hope*

Contrary to imaginary hope, realistic hope is followed with actions in efforts to make it become a reality.

Note on a Strategy to Obtain Hope

The goal + at least five reasons why you want that goal + read these reasons every day = Hope

3- *Conditions of Accomplishing Goals*

- Really want it.
- Make an internal decision that you want to achieve that goal.
- Learn how to achieve the goal (ask experts or people with experience)
- Take action
- Be committed and dedicated

Hope will change into a goal-goal. It will change into thinking of possibilities. Thinking of possibilities will become something you believe. Your belief will become what you want, and you will meet your goal.

4- *Keys to Success*

a) Motivation

In order to achieve your goals, a vital key you must have is motivation. This is what pushes humans. You can learn strategies for success.

How Do You Get Motivation?

- You must want it badly.
- You must ignore all the signs that tell you to not do this or that. Listen to the signs that tell you "you should" in a positive way all the time.

b) Types of Motivation

- Motivation of life
- Motivation from people (not as strong)

    – From books

    – From friends and family

- Motivation from yourself (strongest)

    – The five senses

    – Movement of the body

    – How badly you want it

    – Focusing on your goal

    – Reinforcing positive; make connections to good memories and things you've achieved

    – Breathing

    – Make up your mind, and your body will follow

    – Good statements

    – Focus on and remember your deadline

5- *Past Achievements as an Example*

Every person has a story. Everyone wants to make life better. If you need to achieve your goals, you need to recall your past achievements, mimic that mood, and live it as if it is the present.

a) Remember the past

b) Types of breathing

    – Interval breathing (ten seconds of inhaling, five seconds of exhaling)

    – Heavy breathing (strong inhalation and exhalation)

    – stretching of muscles

    – Bringing in arms closer to chest (inhalation) and extending them away (exhalation)

    – Bringing in closer (down) and up (away) from chest

- Arms extending to the right and left (ten seconds of inhalation and exhalation)
- Bringing in closer (down) and up (away) from chest with tilt to the sides
- Running in place
- Positive thinking and speech
- Drinking water and eating a healthy diet

c) Reasons for Sadness

Sadness can come from nowhere. You might have information in the back of your mind, and that is slowly affecting you, such as someone bullying you without you knowing.

The Unconscious Mind

d) Thinking of solutions to get rid of negativity

If you help someone, picture that person in a positive situation. The gift from Allah looks as if it is a problem. In fact, it is a gift from Allah to challenge you to be better.

e) Location of Knowledge.

Have a love of reading and writing. Listen to motivational speaking in the car, or listen to something positive on the radio. Watch knowledgeable channels on TV. All of these things give you positive thoughts.

Levels of Personality

Believing in yourself and your skills creates a difference, and your strengths and skills build your personality.

Levels of Career	Levels of Personality
1) 7% of this affects you 2) Not as important	1) 93% of your strengths 2) How you treat yourself (very Important) 1) Focus on your decision-making skills 2) Skills to prevent bad beliefs 3) Skills for handling life's trials/ hardships

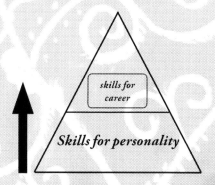

Time Wasted in Life

→ Research shows that humans spend on average:
- 7 years in the washroom
- 5 years waiting for various things
- 1,000 hours in the car
- 120 hours brushing their teeth
- 8 seconds with their children
- 6 years eating
- 1 year opening unimportant messages
- 12 minutes with one's spouse
- 20 minutes reading

→ Research shows that youths under 18 years old spend around 45 hours watching in a week.

→ Research shows that adults from 18 years old to 6 years spend 12 hours watching TV each week.

> **Note:** *Human power can generate electricity for a small country for a week straight.*

Maintaining and Preserving Hope

a) Fusing Hope with Actions

<u>Success Barriers</u>
Fear:

of failure
of the unknown
of rejection
of being a joke
of loss

b) Prolonging and Procrastination

• **The Law of Pressure and Accumulation**

Definition: The presence of a series of problems, and the sequential occurrence of negative events. You end up with self-pressure, intense self-pressure, or chronic self-pressure.

> **Note:** The five senses accommodate programmability in the brain. Changing any variable in your equation of your personal experience changes the whole equation and the whole experience. There is no failure; there are only experiences and experiments. Sometimes you win.

Sometimes I learn: You must have a plan, you must organize that plan. You must find reasons to choose this plan in the head of your plans. And then, you must put that plan into action. This allows you to proceed with success.

- **Optimism**

> **Note:** *Avoid looking for negatives in a positive situation. Any repetitive action you display will be seen by yourself and other people everywhere. A negative approach results in a negative life; a positive approach results in a positive life. The intention within becomes behavior. Predicting a situation (negatively, or positively) results in attracting what might result in the situation. For instance, if one thinks that his house is bound to be robbed, at that very moment he would have sent mental messages to the robbers in the surrounding area.*

Goals are either short term or long term. Short-term goals are terminated as soon as they are achieved. A long-term goal is an endless goal that continues throughout time. For instance, a long-term goal could be bodybuilding. A short-term goal could be getting a haircut.

How to Get Motivation

Ask yourself:

- Where am I?
- Where do I want to go?
- Why do I want to I pursue?
- When do I want it?
- When I get there, what do I do next?

> ***Note***: A human's energy either dissipates with no apparent usefulness or is used to achieve goals.

II. Values, Construction Values, and How to Make Decisions through Values

Being Outstanding and Enjoying; Serenity Allows Achievement

> **Note:** Consciousness leads to discovery, discovery leads to progress, and progress leads to making a connection between happiness and pain. If the result doesn't satisfy you, first change the equation that resulted in the experience.

Your Achievements from Your Values

Production leads to achievement, which in turn leads to happiness. Happiness leads to four results.

1) Your self-appreciation increases.
2) Your self-image is improved in front of people, and that gives life meaning
3) Self-accomplishment
4) Self-trust.

The Brain's Method of Dealing with Data and Information

The conscious brain can focus on about seven pieces of information. However, the subconscious brain can assimilate two million pieces of information per second. You must be able to differentiate between abilities and capabilities. Capabilities change and develop through time. Abilities are unlimited. For instance, you cannot blame your five senses (considered to be abilities) as a reason for your failure. However, you can blame your ignorance, because you did not allocate time to study.

a) Sequence of a Subconscious Brain

– Deeply ingrained values
– Beliefs
– Conscience
– Feelings
– Behavior
– Results and success in life

Values + Motives = Enthusiasm

Values are the reason behind behavior. Pay attention to the inner notifier, your conscience.

b) Values

Values are the roots of a personality. They are the roots of motives. They are the roots of behavior. Values help you think, and thinking entails the presence of a functional brain. After all of these, behavior surfaces.

What indicates a negative and what indicates a positive?

1) You must have values.
2) You must have belief.
3) You must have personal principals and an aspect toward something.
4) With conscience, all of these things are attached to self-concept.

How are values formed?

1) Parents (family)
   – From birth to age 7, 90% of values are normal values

-   From age 7 to age 9, 95% of values are emotional values
2) Social surroundings
3) School
4) Friends
5) Media and social media

c) **The Seven Pillars of Balanced Values**

> It was an imagination, then a thought, then a possibility. The
> nit became a reality not an imagination.

-   ***Examples of Famous People Who Did the Impossible to Achieve Their Goals***

– The Wright Brothers

The Wright brothers, Orville and Wilbur, were two American brothers, inventors, and aviation pioneers who are generally credited with inventing, building, and flying the world's first successful airplane.

– Martin Luther King Jr.

Martin Luther King Jr. was an American Baptist minister and activist who was a leader in the African American Civil Rights Movement. He is best known for his role in the advancement of civil rights using nonviolent civil disobedience based on his Christian beliefs.

– Mahatma Gandhi

Mohandas Karamcheand Gandhi was the preeminent leader of the Indian independence movement in British-ruled India.

– Nelson Mandela

Nelson Rolihlahla Mandela was a South African anti-apartheid revolutionary, politician, and philanthropist who served as president of South Africa from 1994 to 1999. He was the country's first black chief executive, and he was the first elected in a fully representative democratic election.

Hypnotherapy: A form of psychotherapy used to create subconscious change in a patient in the form of new responses, thoughts, attitudes, behaviors, or feelings.

The Seven Pillars of Balanced Values

1) **Spirituality**
2) **Health**
3) **Personality**
4) **Family**
5) **Socialization**
6) **Career**
7) **Money**

These things together compose happiness. Losing any part of them results in depression and the loss of self-confidence.

1) **Spirituality**
   - Obeying the creator of the universe, and obeying the prophet
   - Loving yourself the way you are
   - Loving your parents
   - Loving your siblings
   - Loving people

> **Note:** Before giving, happiness; while giving, happiness; after giving, spiritual power.

2) Family

- Spiritual balance is fundamental in familial relationships. The purity of self helps the presence of strong family ties.
- Taking care of your health because it is fundamental in conserving your strength, which leads to you being able to serve your family even better.

> **Note:** The family is of high value, and you can't give up on them under any circumstances.

The Traditional Method in Marital Relationships

- Attraction and admiration
- Accepting positives and negatives
- Engagement
- Get accustomed with each other
- Enter in a comparative state (both sides will start comparing each other to other people who set a better example).
- Feelings become imbalanced
- The first mistake (from any side)
- Comparing the past and the present (relationship history)
- Exit the relationship
- "We make a living by what we get, but we make a life by what we give." —Winston Churchill

Steps to Achieving Success

1) Imagination
2) Strong belief in the idea
3) Clear plan
4) Self-belief
5) Goals
6) Results and achieving success

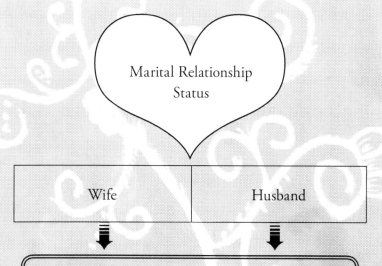

In this stage, they will have a common space between them, and a third person will be created from a group of compromises. This is a mixture including both of them.

The concept of a successful family
- A spiritual life
- A healthy life
- An agreement and love between both
- A familial positive atmosphere

How to Discuss Problems in Cases of Disputes between a Couple

The Challenge

When you and your spouse discuss a problem, do you seem to end up further apart than when you started the conversation? If so, you can improve the situation.

First, though, there are a few things you should know about the different communication styles of men and women.

1) Women usually prefer to talk out problem before hearing a solution. In fact, sometimes talking is the solution.
2) Men tend to think in terms of solutions.

What You Can Do

- For Husbands
  1) Practice empathetic listening. Allow her to express herself and display her frustration; because sometimes a listening ear is all she needs.
  2) The next time you discuss a problem with your wife, resist the urge to give unsolicited advice. Make eye contact and focus on what she is saying.
  3) Nod in agreement and repeat the gist of what she says, to show that you get the point.

- For Wives
  1) Say what you need. Express yourself to your husband and let him know that you need someone to talk to.

2) If your husband prematurely offers solutions, do not conclude that he is being insensitive. He is likely trying to lighten your load.

- For Both

We tend to treat others the way we want to be treated. However, in order to discuss problems effectively, you need to consider how your spouse would like to be treated.

> Pick the right time and the right place, and choose the right words to say.

3) **Health**
    a) Leaving negative habits
    b) Eating healthily
    c) Positive thinking (healthy thinking)
    d) Deep breath (helps you relax and improves activity)
    e) Stretch muscles through exercising and constant body movement
4) **Personality**
    a) Vision
    b) Constant improvement
    c) Self-belief (capabilities and abilities)

- Recognition and understanding the concept of reason and result, in which every action you do has its reasons and results as a consequence.

Habits

The brain works by registering a habit. The brain stores that habit, and in the end, it becomes part of your personality.

For instance, when a person says, "I'm edgy," in reality he isn't edgy, because every child was born collected. Have you ever seen a five-year-old child demanding a cigarette to calm himself down after a surgery?

5) Socialization

a) Help people out (volunteer)
b) Meet new people
c) Build up your conversational skills by engaging with other people
d) Flexibility with people
e) Honestly
f) Ethics and morals
g) Work with a team (teamwork)
h) Independent work

6) Career and Money

a) Satisfaction and enjoyment
b) Focusing on a goal
c) Excellence
d) Flexibility
e) Socialism
f) Self-confidence
g) Reading and self-development
h) Unity with success, in which you and success become one person

The Fruit of Love and Forgiveness

Note: The human generates about sixties ideas in one minute, and 80 percent of these thoughts are negative thoughts. To achieve self-balance, you must forgive people, which will also result in you achieving happiness.

Some misconceptions among people state that forgiveness is a weakness rather than a strength. However, it is definitely a strength. Some people believe that forgiveness makes you an insult-receptive person.

Being Unforgiving Has Drawbacks

1) Negative feeling
2) Continuity in being unforgiving elevates this negative thought
3) Self-pressure
4) Adapting negative behavior
5) Increase in heart rate
6) Increase of adrenaline, which negatively impacts the body(e.g., fatigue)
7) Nightmares

Forgiving Has Advantages

You have a sense of serenity, happiness, and satisfaction. Always forgive yourself, your parents, and your siblings. If anybody does anything appreciable toward you, immortalize that. However, if anybody does anything unappreciable, forgive and forget. You must be generous—especially in time, money, and knowledge.

A Reassuring Self Includes	Results
1) Forgiveness	1) Self-soothe
2) Love	2) Self-acceptance
3) Tenderness	3) Wisdom
4) Generosity	4) Happiness
5) Strife	5) Living contemporarily
6) Trust	
7) Understanding	
8) Humbleness	
9) Education	
10) Patience	
11) Honesty	
12) Good Deeds	

An Evil Self Includes	Results
1) Hatred	1) Self-pressure
2) Jealousy	2) Self-acceptance
3) Comparison	3) Unjustified anxiety
4) Anger	4) Loss of life control
5) Lies	5) Depression
6) Arrogance	6) Lives in the Sad Past
7) Doubt	

Types of Brains

1) An analyzing brain receives power and converts it into human production. It is responsible for information, calculations, logic, and maintaining things—for instance, science, numerals, and names.
2) An emotional brain is a bunch of feelings. In this type of brain, there is no information, and neither there is power. However, it is ignited with instincts and lust.

What Are the Reasons for Failure?

1) Depression
2) Frustration
3) Anxiety
4) Tension
5) Loneliness
6) Unproductive

The explanation of the above states of the human being
1) Avoiding change
2) Refusing personal development

Note: If there is no way, I will make a way.

Personal, inner thoughts are the reason for outward actions and thoughts. What is the meaning of the control concept? You have been told that you've lost your job. Why be angry pissed off or annoyed?

Use the energy of anxiety, and use your time, to find another job. Make use of your time by studying or getting to know another passenger.

Anxiety and tension will give you nothing but will complicate your conditions and make them worse. Do not let negative remarks affect you. Your positive reaction will not spoil your day, and the negative reaction will lead to losing your friends or getting fired from your job, or even cause you to become nervous and exhausted. You can suffer from disease or lack of sleep.

His mind waves:(1) =Beta, (2) = Alpha, (3) = Theta, (4) = Delta

Sleep her stage name Alpha

This is used by suggesting hypnotherapy, stage alpha, when you exhale longer than you inhale.

He repeated more than once, with open eyes and with the inspiration, exhaling slowly and closed in kind. Afterward, you will feel like you want to sleep.

Nonresistance in order to sleep examples shut eyes hard for sleeping or going to watch TV or eat some food.

The brain is like a child: if it's familiar with something, it will ask you to do it every time.

> *Note:* You must be careful about things you make. Make the right decision. Make the right choice.

Be the official of all your actions. If you did not bear the responsibility of your choices, you will face so many problems.
- Self-blame firmly so that you flog flogged
- Criticism from others sharply
- Comparing yourself to others; after sharp criticism, you feel you are less than others
- Complaints
- Procrastination

Cleaning Resin

Inhale clean air and walk through either in parks or in the garden for ten minutes or more on a daily basis. The uses of negative and positive link until they reach the rush does not accept the seriousness of the matter, which is doing the doubt.

> *Note:* Negative and positive links involve still feeling things that you do. It's a sense that either it's inconvenient or that your life makes you feel a sense of happiness and aliveness.

Add new activities that were not in your business before the schedule.

Be Creative

Dive into the depths of the ocean and climb the high mountains in search of the true meaning of life. There is no meaning of life for lost dreams, and in the absence of lost dreams for man.

High volume makes the nervous system is balanced accumulation law:

One starts with the idea after idea of a second after the accumulation of through and feelings then show them. The results appear in the ignition of the emotional mind, an increased heart rate and blood pressure, change in general temperature, and rapid breathing.

- The negative results or positive results
- Thing so beloved by girls
- Smile because it makes the girls fall in love
- Light-hearted young man

Courtesy

Some people could have thought it was a lie, but not until you get to love.

Convergence of Tastes

If you love the same things she loves, you will not be deemed a passing coincidence such as youth.

Thinking, but rather be viewed by a signal from the Lord of the worlds as future wife.

Your Smell

- Bathing; maintain hygiene
- The use of distinctive perfume
- Stylish shoes and white teeth
- Cooks are more men's line; he said the trap with the help of your life
- A young man who loves children is like an angel
- Ground for girls, and it shows you the perfect father
- Encourage your partner
- Show interest in the work
- Attention to the words of the tape is very important
- Spinning paralyze sophisticated
- Establish a strong relationship with the family

Printed in the United States
By Bookmasters